торой.

Билет

ЕННЫЙ

ПНЫЙ ЗАЕМЪ 1917 ГОДА,

о Правительства отъ 11-го Августа

Urgent *2nd* Class

DEUTSCHER RUNDFLUG 1925

B·Z·-PREIS DER LÜFTE

Urgent 2nd Class

CREATING CURIOUS COLLAGE, DUBIOUS DOCUMENTS,

AND OTHER ART FROM EPHEMERA

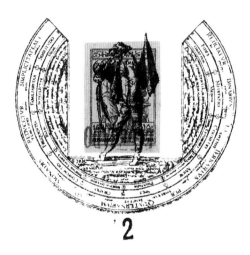

NICK BANTOCK

CHRONICLE BOOKS

SAN FRANCISCO

Many thanks to Joyce Greig, who helped make this book.

Library of Congress Cataloging-in-Publication Data available.

ISBN 0-8118-4305-X

Manufactured in China.

Book Design: Jacqueline Verkley

10 9 8 7 6 5 4 3 2 1

Chronicle Books LLC
85 Second Street
San Francisco, California 94105
www.chroniclebooks.com

for mom

Contents

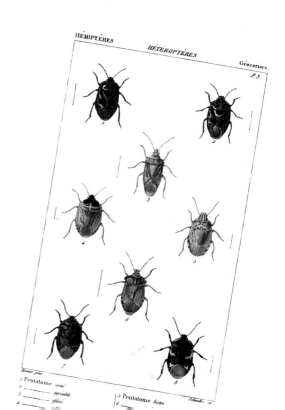

Monnié fdut

1 Pentatome orné
2 _____ agréable
3 _____ effacé
4 _____

5 Pentatome bistre
6

Schindr sc.

Introduction

Yet for better or for worse we love things that bear the marks of grime, soot, and weather, and we love the colors and the sheen that call to mind the past that made them.
—Jun'ichirō Tanizaki, *In Praise of Shadows*, 1977

Imagine a young woman sitting in the accounts payable department of an Italian trading office in 1910. The afternoon is dragging interminably. She drifts into a reverie and starts to doodle on the invoice in front of her. Like many educated people of the time, she can draw with reasonable competence. She sketches the faces of her coworkers as she remembers them at the recent New Year's fancy-dress party. The result of this graphic detour is a fascinating mixture of period commerce and art.

Is it important that she never actually put pencil to paper and that it is you or I who decides to act out her part for her? Is the invoice worth less because we have created a fiction over a fact? Surely what matters is the degree of poignant emotion evoked by the resultant piece of paper.

I love the idea of a creativity that honors the effects of time and makes mischief with history. Growing up in a society where hard, cold, and shiny are often highly valued, I find myself gravitating toward the opposite. Snow-blinded by bleached white paper, I crave smoky patina and shadowy aged surfaces.

Urgent 2nd Class is a handbook for those who wish to learn how to embellish and

[*Contrived Crash Card*]

found material to create curiosities like faux mail, dubious documents, and the other anomalies found in this book are legion. A volume of this moderate size, however, cannot cover them all and, instead, offers a sample of the ways in which ephemera can be expanded upon.

By *ephemera* I mean torn maps, tattered letters, timeworn etchings, out-of-date banknotes, old game boards, redundant labels, near-worthless manuscripts, and other unloved scraps of paper. In short I refer to the disheveled, foxed, creased, and half-burnt leftovers of bygone eras.

In the following pages I will show what happens when you add to this ephemera drawings, postage stamps, cancels, petroglyphs, hand lettering, labels, rubber stampings, and virtually anything else close at hand. A fascinating world is brought to life that never quite was but almost might have been. A place of visual poetry where communication can be either trustworthy . . . or not.

You will notice that this book slips back and forth between seeking and selecting ephemera and the various techniques involved in adding to these found items. This is mostly because the method of working that I propose tends to be "chicken and eggish"—the finding directs the making and the making feeds the finding. Some chapters concentrate on specific techniques such as drawing or

tamper with old documents, envelopes, and other ephemeral scraps. Its intended purpose is to bring into focus an art form that has barely been identified, let alone described.

I hope this volume begins to remedy that lapse, as well as encourage and stimulate innate creativity.

The techniques involved in altering

[*Filthy Luker*]

rubber stamping, whereas others, like the sections on postcards or games, focus more on untouched artifacts.

To be honest, it makes little difference to me whether I end up adding to a piece or not. I get the same excitement from hunting down, selecting, and giving a home to these items as I do from physically manipulating them. When I put something I have chosen in a file drawer or in a frame, its meaningfulness to me comes from its elegance of composition, its humor, or its universality.

Everything in *Urgent 2nd Class* was cheap! The bits and pieces came from junk stores, garage sales, online auctions, storerooms, and sometimes garbage piles. There is no guilt or worry over the destruction of museum-quality material because nothing here cost more than ten dollars. This figure indicates not miserliness but merely a boundary that allows me to know that whatever I do I am not defacing something of real historical value. If damaged or dull ephemera can be given a new purpose, so be it.

The concept of order and chaos overlapping one another intrigues me. Whether it be vine-engulfed ruins or a new edifice emerging out of the jungle, there is something stimulating about the codependence of the contrived and the organic. Maybe that's why so many of us feel affection for weather-beaten,

[*Chicago World's Fair Card Box*]

barnacle-encrusted ship's figureheads or ancient sculptures with lopped off arms. As Walt Whitman put it, "The weed will win in the end." It's a pleasing idea, not because it takes pleasure in the ultimate demise of civilization, but because it is an affirmation of change.

I'm inclined to think that we, the children of the latter portion of the twentieth century, bought the Emperor's New Clothes when it came to art philosophy. We've accepted a line of thought implying that aesthetics are purely a matter of individual taste and personal whim. Ironically, in so doing, we've laid ourselves open to be led by cheap fad. Though it may not be a popular view, I believe that there is a universal aesthetic, an internal visual balance mechanism that defines beauty and composition. This means that the opposite is also true—equality is admirable, but why kid ourselves that ugly doesn't exist. Awareness of balance and harmony is something that needs to be worked on and developed within us.

As much as I respect the well-lit giants of the Renaissance, I'm not making an elitist plea for "high art." On the contrary, this book tries to show that good art can be found in many a dark corner. It just has to be discovered, played with, nurtured, and appreciated. Only when we develop a strong sense of aesthetic within the everyday will we avoid having crude and clumsy uglification served to us in the name of art and personal taste.

So what am I encouraging you to make? Not forgeries or fakes. There is no pretense to hide the concept of fantasy and no attempt to suggest something is other than what it appears. What I want to show is that a little wit and guile can move us backward and forward within an artifact's history, giving us an enhanced sensitivity toward the archaic and the ever malleable. In so doing, we allow ourselves to develop a creativity rooted in something stronger than the transience of fashion.

If I can help other artists find their own personal species of outsider art, maybe we'll further widen the eyes of all those who take delight in the visual world.

[*Heartburn Matches*]

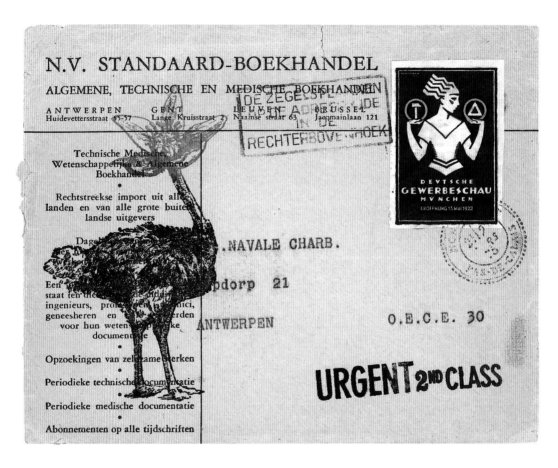

[*Ostrich Flower*] A rubber stamp and a Cinderella (see Stamp chapter) can be enough to change an envelope's whole personality.

< 6 >

Faux Mail

I can't make up my mind if mail art has to pass though the post in order to make it "official." If it does, anyone depositing their precious work in the postbox runs the risk of losing it to the postal ether. If the art doesn't have to be posted, what defines it as mail art—the fact that it's attached to an envelope? That seems an incredibly open-ended definition. My interest is a bit more specific: faux mail. Faux mail, according to me, is an envelope that has artwork added to it after it has already been though the mail and earned its maturity.

By working with old used envelopes, I find I'm dealing with a form of pre-cast truth—something that has already received its markings and cancellations and gone through a rite of passage. It bears its history as a duelist carries his scars. Of course, I could simply leave

these envelopes as pieces of postal memorabilia, but where's the entertainment in that? I like to view an old envelope as an interesting starting point with grounds for improvement or, to be more provocative, as an opportunity to tamper with the mail. The best examples of faux mail are not merely decorative but reactive to the surface they reside on. They express a thought, a feeling, or an idea in both their style and their content.

Mind you, there are times when altering a piece is unnecessary. I found two Chinese red-stripe folded letters and tried to improve on the first by adding a canceled stamp, but it didn't need it; in fact, the stamp took something away from the letter's simple perfection. So the second letter (page 10), I left completely untouched.

[*Lettuce-Tailed Skunk Mail*]

Carta Postal

Sr. Director de **La Industria Azucarera**

Calle de Plumereros, 103.

Correo apartado 17.   **LIMA.**

by ship's catapult

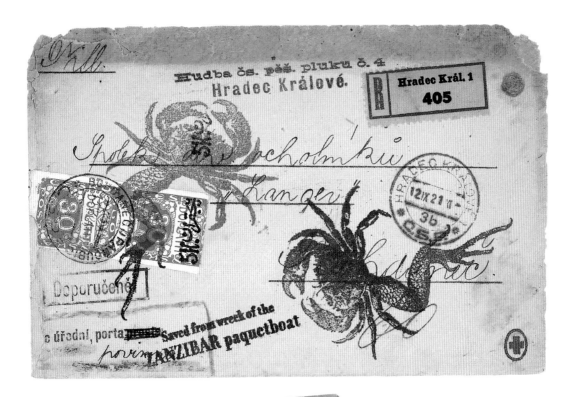

[*Fishtail and Crabs*] What if an iguana-tailed fish might deliver pneumatic mail or a pair of lizard-footed crabs could leave their shadows on an envelope?

FACING PAGE: [*Lizard Lima*] Most South and Latin American countries once produced very pleasing preprinted letter cards. The lizard rubber stamping and the catapult mark help give the impression of a missive from a ship's anthropologist.

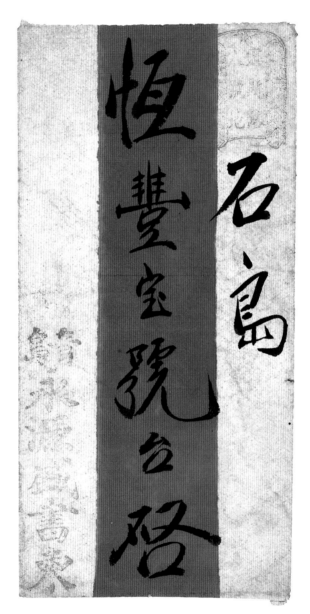

[*Red Stripe*] Unaltered!

[*Airships and Seaplane*]

ABOVE: I joined together sections of a 1920s Russian poster, and then added the airship stamps, the cancels, and the address.

LEFT: The Canadian airmail came with the beaver, but I added the end-of-the-world notification.

< 11 >

ABOVE: [*The Postman's Nightmare*] Mail doesn't always reach its destination. Sometimes it chases its intended recipient all round the globe. This piece of sheer chaos made a few detours, but the majority of its zigzag touring was down to me.

LEFT: [*Forward from Egypt*] I added the orange stamp and the pyramid cancel along with the black forwarding flap, which came off the back of a Victorian studio photographer's card.

FACING PAGE: [*The Harem Window*] An ex-invoice envelope frames an Ouled Nail dancer.

< 13 >

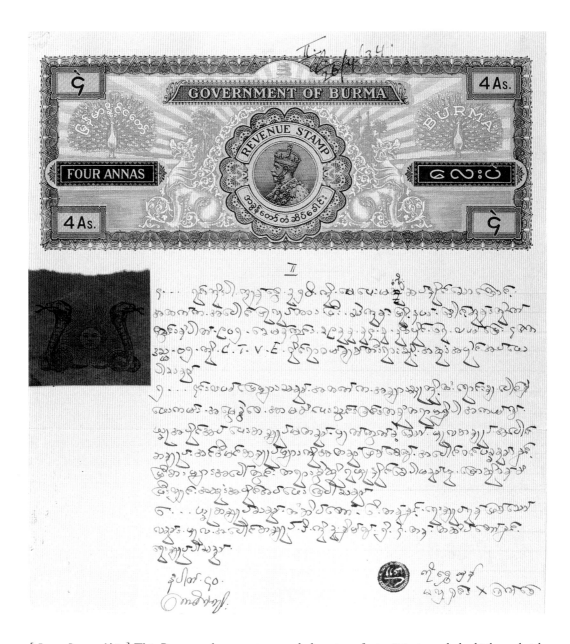

[*Burma Revenue Note*] This Burmese document seemed almost perfect—it just needed a little snakeish charm.

< 14 >

Dubious Documents

Invoices, business forms, passports, visas, marriage and death certificates: there's almost no end to institutional and commercial paperwork. Like most people, I get bogged down by the weight of having to respond to this avalanche of dry wordage. The occasional disrespectful riposte directed toward authority can be most satisfying, especially if the body in question is a defunct Empire—with no one left to complain about any irreverences.

By their nature, official documents take themselves rather seriously, which makes them perfect for a little teasing. This can mean adding an unexpected image to the text or simply putting artifacts alongside one another for unexpected comparison. The addition doesn't have to be blatant; some of these papers need close inspection to see what you can insert in the small print.

For some reason there seems to be a proliferation of nineteenth-century eastern European legal documents in Vancouver, where I live. In a few years they'll be gone—distributed more evenly across the universe—but for now I can buy them cheaply. It was tempting to fill this whole chapter with multiple variations of elegantly stamped Austro-Hungarian administration details and their fine handwriting. However, as in the rest of the book, I'm trying to show the broadest of stylistic possibilities, nationalities, subject matters, and techniques, so I've kept the Magyar manuscripts to a minimum.

[*The Tu Cany Lion of Stanley Park*]

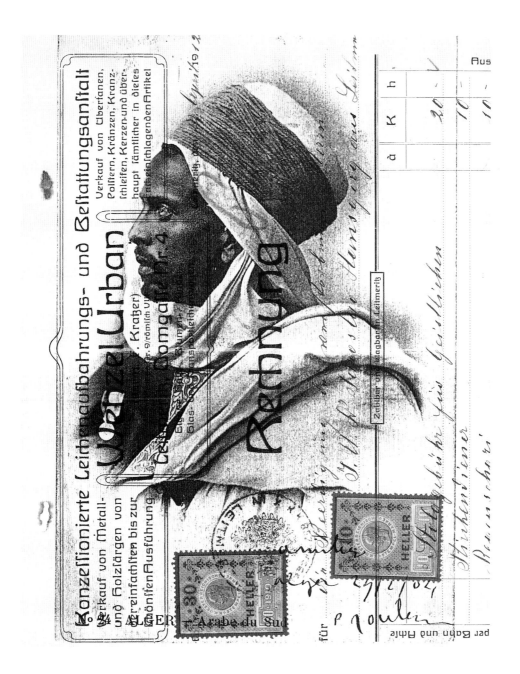

[*Alger*] The image doesn't have to relate directly to the text. In this case the mysteriousness of the link is part of the attraction.

FACING PAGE: [*Organic Invoice*] If the bills aren't paid, one tends to get overrun. Black line art was copied onto the document, then colored with watercolor and fixed.

< 18 >

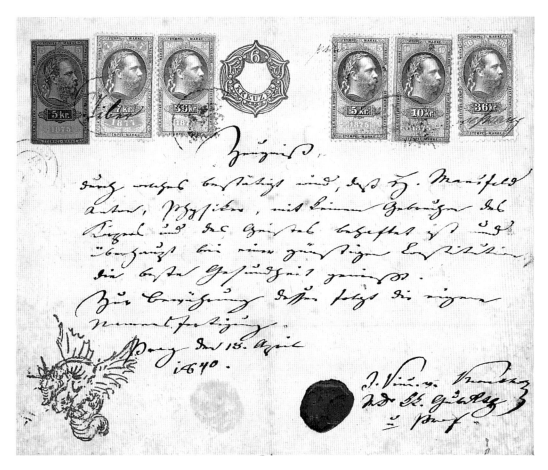

[*The Emperor's Doppelgängers*] The full row of Austrian fiscal stamps (there was only one to start) have been added to aid and abet the document's air of importance.

FACING PAGE: [*Bird of Prey*] A French distiller and his (rubber-stamped) delivery boy, plus a Swedish fiscal.

FOLLOWING PAGE: [*Acid Rain*] A factory document is given an element of foreboding by color-copying an old chemist's bottle into its heart. I overlaid a sheet of clean paper and rubbed it with wintergreen. That sucked out the surface ink and left the bottle looking like part of the original sheet.

Účty bankovní a poštovního úřadu šekového
Živnostenská banka v Praze.
Filiáka České eskomptní banky ve Warnsdorfě
Poštovní úřad šekový v Praze čís 59382.

Tovární: Lipsko-Gohlis

ZALOŽENO 1882.

Ochranná známka

Tovární ve Warnsdorfu

Oehme & Baier
WARNSDORF (ČECHOSLOVENSKO.)

Ovocné trestě na cukrové zboží, limonády a.t.d.
Ovocné a kořenné výtažky, ovocná aroma zhuštěná.
Eterické oleje, trestě na líhoviny a likéry
Rumové trestě.
Jedu prosté barvy na potraviny všech druhů
jako zboží cukrové, limonádové syrupy,
likéry, líhoviny a.t.d.
Polevy na čokoládu, perník a.t.d. Čistěné benzoe.

Adresa pro telegramy: Oebaier Warnsdorf.
Telefon pro hovory mezimětské: Čís 246.

VE WARNSDORFU, 14. prosince

Čechoslovensko.

Pan

Frant. Tejkl,

továrna na likéry,

St. Zábřeh,

Morava.

Děkujíce Vám za zakázku nám laskavě udělenou, pokládáme si za česť zpraviti Vás o jej
nejpečlivějším vyřízení a dovolujeme si předložiti účet, za jehož obnos
Kč   650.45   nás laskavě uznati račtež.
Doporoučejíce Vám své další služby co nejlépe, znamenáme

s veškerou úctou

ÚČET   Oehme & Baier.

Lhůta = měsíc = neb za hotové = % srážky.
Splatno a žalovatelno ve Warnsdorfu.

ujíce Váš příkaz zaslali jsme na účet Váš i nebezpečí   poštou
dráhou   nevyplacené.

Čís

1 sud brutto 44 kr		120
4 litrů višnové stav	16.=	50
		1
	Kč.	650

Splatno netto kassa při

Činíme Vás pozorna že
k udanění.

24/3 1922

[*Passports*] To me there's something semidraconian about any official government document that contains an ID photo.

< 21 >

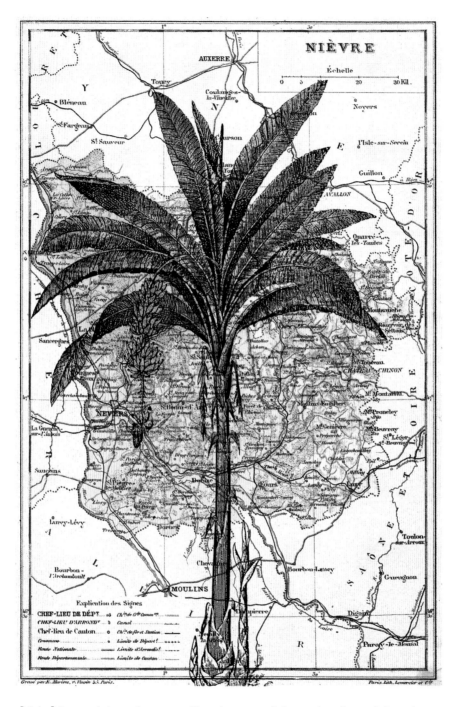

[*Palm*] I copied this palm onto a French map and then colored it with liquid watercolor.

Maps

A couple of years ago I was in Denver looking around a store that sold old maps. The beautiful historical gems of cartography were either carefully framed or otherwise sealed from the elements. Even the oldest maps were amazingly well preserved and appropriately expensive. After ten minutes of quiet ogling, I sidled up to the store owner and sheepishly asked if he had anything damaged and badly aged. He looked at me as though I were asking for a dry crust of bread in a five-star restaurant. I explained that I wasn't a collector but I wanted the material for making artwork (I tend to pump up what's left of my English accent in cases like this because it helps portray me as eccentric rather than lunatic).

This approach can lead to one of two responses: dealers consider my intentions sacrilegious (even though they will probably end up trashing the kind of stuff I want) or they become curious and want to know more about my creative endeavors. In this particular case the latter variety of conversation ensued, and after a short while the owner descended into his basement, rumbled around, and returned with a few small, heavily foxed maps. I glanced through the pile and plucked out a plum: a brown ink map of Egypt from the late 1700s. It was torn and distinctly worse for wear and at one point had been folded so that the left and right sides of the map had ghosted themselves onto their opposite halves. I loved it!

I inquired about price, and the now-affable owner offered it to me at a minute fraction of the cost of its elegant relatives on the walls. I handed him a small bill, thanked him profusely, and departed the establishment as pleased as Punch.

Sadly, good fortune like that doesn't happen often, but it shouldn't stop you from trying. Most of my map art comes down to lesser items found in junk stores and garage sales—things that need a fair bit of work to invigorate.

[*Egypt in Denver*]

< 23 >

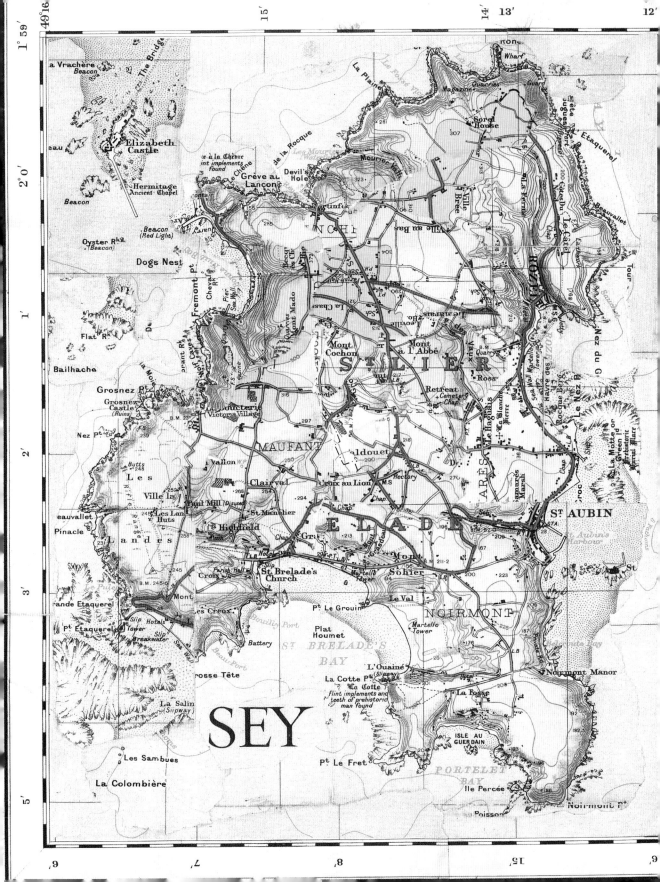

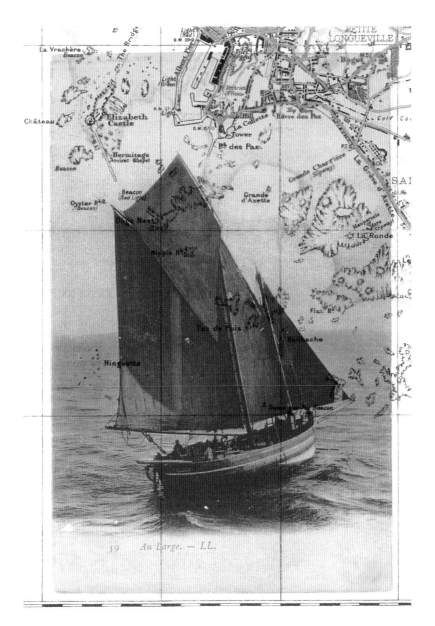

[*Layover*] Using the spare center section of the Sey map, I made an acetate overlay and placed the coast outline on top of the image of the boat.

FACING PAGE : [*The Isle of Sey*] Look carefully—this is not quite what it seems. Using a large Ordnance Survey map from the 1940s, I tore small sections of the coastline and rebuilt a new, small island out of the pieces. NB: Sey is yes backwards, and the middle of the island has a town called St. Lier.

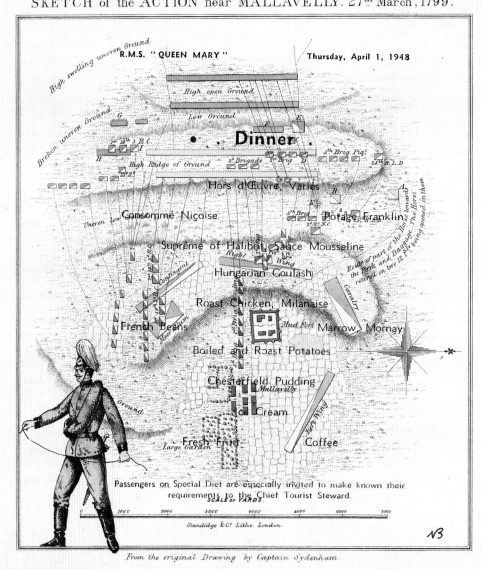

SKETCH of the ACTION near MALLAVELLY. 27th March, 1799.

From the original Drawing by Captain Sydenham.

[*The 7th Hungarian Goulashers*] The merging of two completely unrelated items can often instigate a very interesting outcome, like the battle plan that has been married to a 1948 menu from the Queen Mary ocean liner. It would seem that the incursion of the coffee has taken on a potentially devastating strategic, military importance . . .

Could I have conceived such a bizarre document from scratch? Not a hope in hell! It had to come from messing around with the hodgepodge of "stuff" that inhabits my studio.

< 26 >

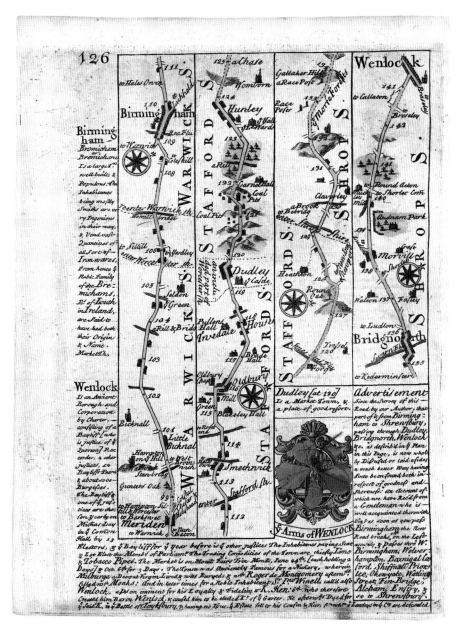

[*The Shropshire Road*] This strip map of an English thoroughfare I bought in Australia. I liked everything about it apart from the heraldic shield, so I superimposed a pressed four-leafed clover.

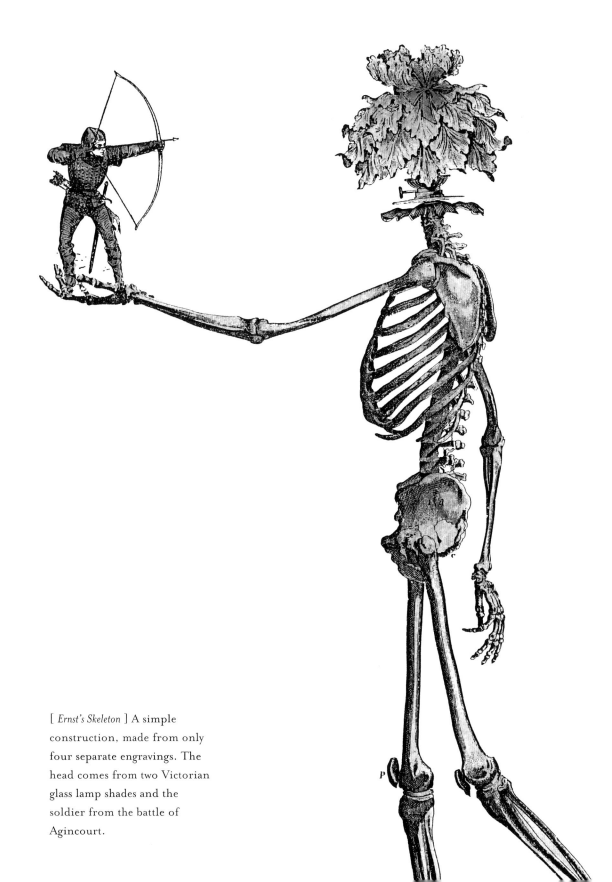

[*Ernst's Skeleton*] A simple
construction, made from only
four separate engravings. The
head comes from two Victorian
glass lamp shades and the
soldier from the battle of
Agincourt.

Engravings

In 1919 Max Ernst began to cut and paste together line engravings from lurid novels and mechanical manuals, using the disembodied parts of the illustrations to make new pictures of a dreamlike and surreal nature. The appeal to him, and other artists that followed, was not only the speed of the method but also the way in which impulsive decisions and accidents of placement could supplement predictable thinking patterns. Ernst employed the laws of chance to come up with images like a bizarre bird-headed woman and a top-hatted man teaching a mouse to rotate.

Engravings were the main means of representational graphic art, and they were in great abundance until photography muscled them out of the public limelight around the turn of the nineteenth century. You can easily find them in old books and magazines, and they're perfect for creating patchwork dreamscapes.

I've included a couple of examples in this chapter that I constructed to resemble direct descendants of Ernst's work. One is a straightforward piece of gothic humor; the second is more florally whimsical and complex. They have a tighter, more finished look than Ernst's collages but cannot begin to match the jarring impact that his work had on the art-interested public of his day.

Keep in mind that engravings are not the only graphic source material available. Many other types of line art are waiting to be unearthed, from lithographic cartoons to sheet music—any of which could be fated to help you set free a whimsical bird-headed, rodent-circling muse.

[*Deep Sea Thingy*]

[*Fish Music*] The fish are drawn with ink dots over the top of an aging piece of sheet music. It's hard to describe, but there was a certain floating inevitability about this picture, as though it was predetermined.

FACING PAGE: [*The Dodger's Dream*] There are thirty-one different torn pieces that made up this grossly over-the-top Dickensian melodrama.

PLATE 31.

FELIS CALIGATA (The Booted Lynx)
Bruce.   Native of Africa.

PLATE 29.

FELIS CATUS. (The common Wild Cat.)
Edin.ᵗRoy.U.Museum.

[*Tinting Cats*] You will probably pay a lot more for a color engraving than a black-and-white one that you later enliven yourself. Helpful hint—it's better to paint two coats of a lighter wash than one coat that turns out too dark.

FACING PAGE: [*Composing Felines*] In my experience, lions tend to have a Wagnerian hunger for music.

< 32 >

[*Tutonic Merger*] My original intention was to make this image out of just four German banknotes, but it felt too rigid. So I dug around and came up with the tarnished coins. Not quite the same era but geographically sound.

< 34 >

Money

Paper money was first conceived by the Chinese in the seventh century and was called "flying money" for its lightness and ease of transportation. Three centuries later they had a well-developed and relatively smooth system of countrywide exchange. After Marco Polo returned to Europe from China in the thirteenth century, he mentioned this paper money to his contemporaries, who were used to coinage. They laughingly dismissed his story as obvious fantasy. How could anyone use a currency that wasn't valued in terms of the metal it contained?

The Spanish began printing banknotes in 1483, but all of these early occidental issues were destroyed in the Siege of the Moors. When the rest of Europe finally committed itself to paper money, the printing method used was engraving—a technique that not only helped instigate a new era in fine design but also became a major weapon in the battle against forgery (a problem that the Chinese had struggled with from the outset). Governments and printers still go to great lengths to manufacture banknotes that are tough to copy. Up until recent years the combination of watermarked paper and complex machine-tooled engraving gave the authorities the edge on any illicit platemakers. With the advent of sophisticated computers, however, the struggle to keep counterfeit money out of circulation has gradually become more difficult.

When gathering paper money, you can purchase many magnificent items for next to nothing. The German period of high inflation in the 1920s, for example, gave rise to barrowloads of paper money that was virtually worthless, even though the design and coloring were of a high quality.

The facing page shows a collage of four German banknotes, some cut and some torn. It's worth observing the subtly emotional difference one experiences between the sliced and the ripped paper.

[*French Flag*]

[*Orient*] From my box of bruised bills came
these scattered Chinese and Japanese notes.

[*Uncurrency*] A tobacco note for its intense blued paper and muted red type, a section of Soviet scripophily for its orange ink, and a Confederate note for its elaborate engraving.

[*Russia*] The high-value gray-and-white note shows Peter the Great (Catherine was given the lower denomination—a case of rampant patriarchy?). The second and third notes are there for their good looks.

FACING PAGE: [*A Banker's Bond*] I had the photo of a banker for a while. When I got the bond at an antique store, I knew they were made for each other.

< 38 >

Series C

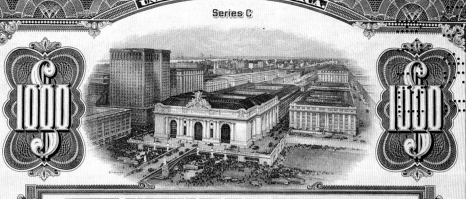

$1000 \qquad 1000$

THE NEW YORK CENTRAL
RAILROAD COMPANY

Refunding and Improvement Mortgage Bond.
Five Per Cent.

Nº **M7621**   Nº **M7621**

The New York Central Railroad Company (hereinafter called the Railroad Company) a corporation of the State of New York, and other states, for value received, hereby promises to pay to bearer, or, if this bond be registered, then to the registered holder hereof, on the first day of October, 2013, at the office or agency of the Railroad Company in the Borough of Manhattan, City of New York, the sum of

One Thousand Dollars,

in gold coin of the United States, of or equal to the standard of weight and fineness as it existed on the first day of October, 1913, and to pay interest thereon from the date hereof at the rate of five per cent per annum, such interest to be payable at such office or agency in like gold coin, semi-annually, on the first day of April and the first day of October in each year until the payment of said principal sum, but only upon presentation and surrender of the coupons therefor hereto attached as they severally mature. This bond is one of a duly authorized issue of Refunding and Im...

Secretary, and coupons ...
Treasurer to be attached hereto. Dated the first day of ... *nineteen hundred and* ... *one.*

The New York Central Railroad Company

by

Attest:

ASSISTANT SECRETARY.   VICE PRESIDENT

[*Boxing a Zulu*] I cut the warrior into equal-sized squares, rotated them, and then I glued them down. Once firm, I covered the picture with a layer of white tissue, coated it with matte medium, and worked colored chalk dust into the surface.

< 40 >

Photographs

In an old container in the corner of a junk store, you might stumble on a photo that seems to come from another world, an image that has slipped through an ethereal crack in the fabric of some sepia universe. The Ogopogo (page 42) certainly comes from that realm. I remember when I first saw it lurking in a cardboard box, waiting for liberation from the company of its dull and ultra-normal inmates. What I like about it is how it looks equally right upside down or downside up.

The photographs in this chapter are old ones possessing an ineffable quality that attracts me. When I find a picture that catches my attention, I want to know why. What is it that sucks me in? I want to see where it wants to go or how far I can push it—like the camel with its head cropped by the mount on page 43. The photo was already interesting because of the sphinx and pyramid, but framing the picture off center suggests the camel's wandering, obstreperous nature.

There is something too complete about most photos, which makes them less penetrable than other ephemera. They need a dose of controlled eccentricity that will alter and personalize them, or, as in the example of the phototransfer (page 46), the picture surface needs to be broken up to give it breathing space.

I tend to split photographs into two categories: family and found. Family includes all photos taken of people or places I know intimately. Generally I do not use this material for art, because it is too close to home. I'm not overly interested in battling internally with where sentimentality ends and nostalgia begins—so I steer clear altogether. For creative purposes I'm more concerned with found material. Because I don't know the story behind these photos (bought, begged, and borrowed), I'm encouraged to use my imagination. I can knock them about without guilt. I'm not defacing my great-great auntie, so I don't have to worry about family ghosts (at least not mine!).

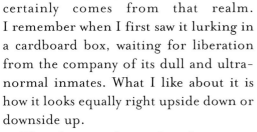

[*The Tunisian Boy*]

85374

[*A Headless Camel*] Shaped Victorian family window mats are still pretty easy to find. The paper tends to be moistureless, so you need to steer clear of runny inks or paints because they'll bleed like crazy.

FACING PAGE: [*Ogopogo*] I wanted the Ogopogo on an appropriate background, so I picked a bark paper and stenciled in his social security number.

< 43 >

[*Directing Traffic*] When you get a photo printed from negative or transparency there is no reason why you can't overlap one on top of the other.

< 44 >

Bird of paradise - HAWAII

Wooden rose - H.wiia

[*Lantern Slides*] I wanted to give the feel of these 1920s glass slides both when they are held up to the light and seen flat on the table, so I had the images scanned and printed, then I carefully re-created and stuck down the brown paper borders and the misspelled labels, which I banged out on my anciently erratic typewriter.

< 45 >

[*Phototransfer*] Color photocopy any image, put it face up, and lay over it white artpaper. Use a cloth to rub acetone on the back of the art paper. When you separate the papers, you'll find that much of the image has transferred from the photocopy to the art paper.

16. SENEGAL — Femme Dahobé   Fortier Photo. Dakar

[*Reverse Transfer*] After photo-transference, the remains of the image still on the donor copy paper can sometimes be as interesting as that on the recipient art paper.

[*Constructing a Fictitious Commemorative*] A. Full-size pencil and wash drawing of steam locomotive.

B. Scaled-down photocopy of drawing. C. Original stamp. D. Camel removed with a scalpel.

E. New stamp with locomotive inserted. F. The newly created stamp on an envelope with a hand cancel.

< 48 >

Stamps

If you add an old postage stamp to a collage, it will automatically place the work in a specific period and region of the world. If you position the stamp with care and consideration, it can also balance the picture out. Don't just plunk the stamp anywhere; arbitrary placement can do more harm than good. I say this because often I notice that a collage or piece of artwork is not properly thought through. There are hundreds of bad compositional placements for every element and only a few good ones. Getting it dead right is part of the effort of practicing good art.

I'll spend a long time choosing a stamp that matches the imagery it's going to join. Then I'll move it around all over the surface, trying out both obvious and unobvious positions, turning it slightly out of kilter, this way and that. When I have the exact position, I mark two corner points, glue, and attach.

As a general rule, if you want stamps that are brightly colored, look for those designed after the mid-1950s. If you want less garish stamps with more emphasis on delicacy of design, seek out issues prior to that period. On pages 50 and 51, you'll find a selection of stamps that cover the full spectrum of styles and regions. As beautiful as they are, none of these stamps is expensive. Many of them you could buy from a stamp store and get change from a quarter. In fact, you can see the whole history of graphic design over the last one hundred fifty years spread over these two pages.

Most stamp stores have a big box of cheap stamps you can root through to get familiar with the wide-ranging choices. Stamps fall into different categories, and it helps to know some of the basic philatelic language. So here's a quick breakdown. *Postal*, for the sending of a letter. *Postage dues*, for letters that don't have enough postage. *Fiscals*, for monetary and legal transactions. *Cinderellas*, for all stamps including advertising that are not post-office issue. Imperforated labels, lacking perforations, for use on airmail and registered letters.

[*A Proof of Three Heads*]

[*Economic Élan*] Apart from the stamps I use in collages, I keep a separate small book of stamps with unusual color combinations. If while working on a picture I find myself slipping into a predictable palette, I consult the book and pick a pair of colors I wouldn't normally think of combining.

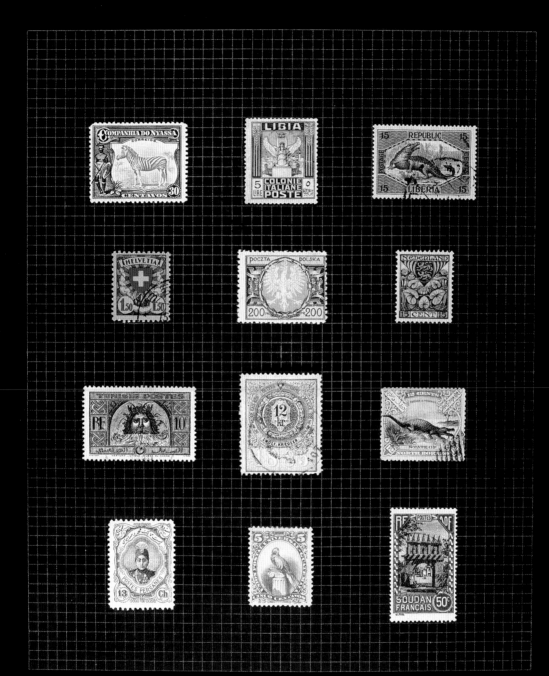

REPÚBLICA DE CHILE
10 No. 91820 10
D Santiago.

R No. 170
SAIGON
PRINCIPAL- 1

República del Ecuador
CORREOS
R 8210

CORREOS DEL PERU
R
Nº 906642

R PENANG A
No 4185

R MALE
No 11040

FRANCEVILLE
9803

LUFTPOST
PAR AVION

AIR MAIL
SWISSAIR
PAR AVION

بالبريد الجوى
AIR MAIL
PAR AVION

PAR AVION
航空郵便

PAR AVION
SCADTA
CORREO AEREO
MANCOMUN

PAPEETE-TAHITI
R 017

PAR AVION
via AIR MAIL
JAL
JAPAN AIR LINES

UÇAK İLE
PAR AVION

AIR MAIL
PAR AVION

ESPAÑA
CORREO AEREO

KLM ROYAL DUTCH AIRLINES
AIR MAIL

AIR MAIL

VIA AEREA

Par Avion
By Air Mail
FORM 2978

VIA
AIR MAIL

[*Cinderellas*] One of the reasons that nonpostal stamps are fairly uncommon is the difficulty in finding a printer with a perforating machine. Please, anyone with a PhD in laser technology, design a cheap, simple (gauge variable) perforating device.

FACING PAGE: [*Airmailed and Registered*] These little labels tend not to be collected or given catalogue value, so if you root around, you'll be able to pick up the odd one here and there. If you're lucky enough to find a whole batch of obscure old ones . . . my birthday is July 14th!

[*Cover Up*] Again three different elements—an embossed album cover, a deco pigskin from a volume of zoology, and a miniature metal replica of a door knocker.

< 54 >

Books and Magazines

The rebuilding of aged, crumbling binding is relatively expensive, so most books slowly disintegrate until they totally fall apart. Therefore, exhausted old tomes provide an almost limitless supply of material for the ephemera arts. From covers, spines, and endpapers to pages and illustrations, everything can be reused. Like a washed-up whale discovered by an Inuit, nothing is wasted!

While I would never dismember a good or rare book, if an old encyclopedia is coming apart on its own, I'm not averse to helping it toward reincarnation. Walk into almost any secondhand bookstore, and you'll find a few tatty but beautiful leather and cloth hardback book covers that are slowly detaching themselves from the body of the book block. A Dickens or a Burns will probably cost you a fair bit, but if you choose something obscure and out of favor, you'll be surprised how little it will set you back.

Then there's the other side of the antiquarian tracks . . . mid-twentieth century detective, sci-fi, and sleaze paperback book covers can be gems in their own right. Like B movies, illustrated pulp-fiction covers range from the magnificently over-the-top to the appallingly bad. Either way, they can be quite special.

I can never make up my mind whether magazines are more closely related to books or to newspapers. At the turn of the nineteenth century, *The London Illustrated News* was really a thin, large-format book with stories by Conan Doyle and the like. As time passed, however, and the attention span of the populace started to shrink, magazines reduced their text content and began filling themselves with graphic images. While this in some small way may have helped contribute to the long-lamented decline of literacy, it has certainly added to the bank of illustrations and photographs readily available in the back of junk stores. And this not a bad thing for those of us who need infinite fodder for our collages.

[*Ex Libris*]

[*The Maid Did It*]
By bringing together these very different covers, a twisted relationship emerges suggesting a bizarre hidden narrative.

WALTER BAKER & CO.
Dorc

TH
LARG
P

HAVE RECEIVED HIGHEST
FROM THE GREAT INDUSTRIAL AND FOOD EXPOSITIONS I
THEIR DELICIOUS BREAKFAST COCOA COSTS LESS

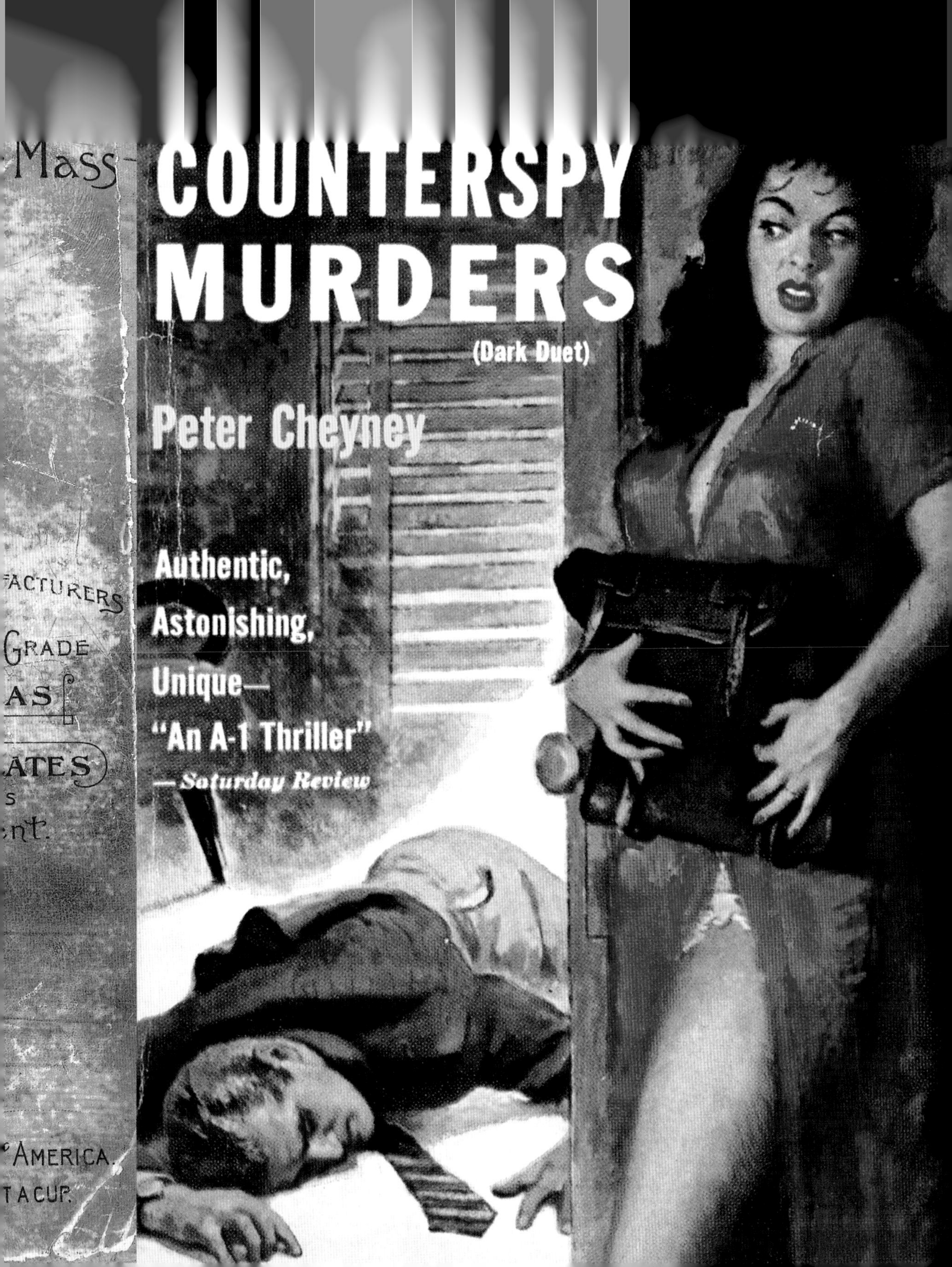

COUNTERSPY MURDERS

(Dark Duet)

Peter Cheyney

Authentic,
Astonishing,
Unique—
"An A-1 Thriller"
—*Saturday Review*

[*Insects and Endpapers*] The spine, the engraving, and the illustration come from three different books. If you select with care, the union can work pretty well.

< 58 >

THE SAME OLD ACT IN THE POLITICAL DRAMA.
Re-enter the Tammany Tiger — Exit the Beautiful Vision of Reform.

[*Puck*] As much as I love the Robin Hood tiger illustration, my favorite part of this cover is the amber color of the withered tape in the top corner.

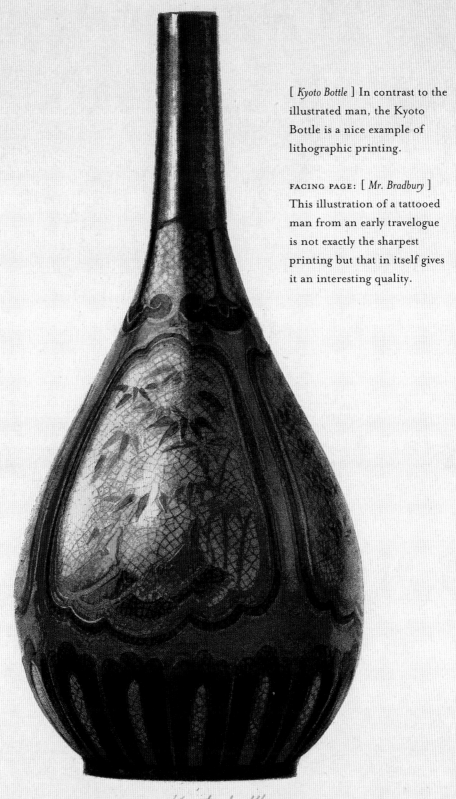

[*Kyoto Bottle*] In contrast to the
illustrated man, the Kyoto
Bottle is a nice example of
lithographic printing.

FACING PAGE: [*Mr. Bradbury*]
This illustration of a tattooed
man from an early travelogue
is not exactly the sharpest
printing but that in itself gives
it an interesting quality.

Kyoto bottle

[*Uncut Matchboxes*] Nearly all small printing jobs were done as repeat images that were ganged together and then cut after the inks had dried.

< 62 >

Commercial Ephemera

How do you begin to explain to someone who doesn't get it, why you think a King Pelican iceberg lettuce crate label is truly stunning? As soon as I saw the label on page 64, I started leaping around with excitement. Its style is clearly of another era, yet it's not the slightest bit dated. There's no real marketing relationship between lettuce and a pelican wearing a crown as far as I can see, which adds to the perfection of the label. It works simply because whatever it's advertising has to be worth getting.

Once I started to look around, I was astounded at how many different products used to put their heart and soul into dramatic and colorful promotion. Matchboxes and matchbooks, cigarette cards, luggage labels, fruit labels, seed packets, travel posters and tickets—the list is endless. I even discovered thirteen great-looking 1920s broom-handle labels— I didn't even know that brooms had labels!

At auction I bought three sheets of uncut Swedish matchbox labels. It was a tough choice which sheet to include, but in the end the "Torpedo" battleship won over the llamas and the tigers. I couldn't resist seeing the eighteen ships chugging remorselessly across the page like still frames from an interminable Andy Warhol movie.

I don't want to get too euphoric here because there was an awful lot of dreary and downright bad commercial art. Nevertheless, it seems ironic that some of the best art of its day can be found within the normally predictable and repetitious world of advertising.

[The Demonic Wine]

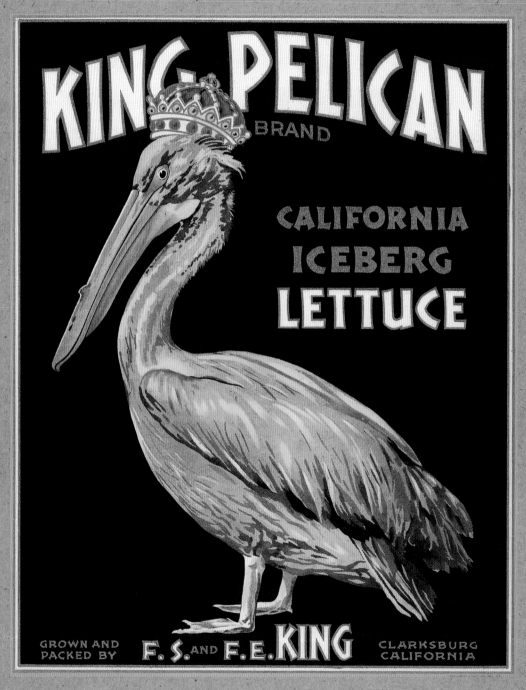

[*Iceberg*] I once heard Marvin Gaye say in an interview that after he recorded "Heard It Through the Grapevine," he had no realization that he had produced something special. I wonder if the King Pelican's illustrator exhibited the same after-the-fact matter-of-factness.

< 64 >

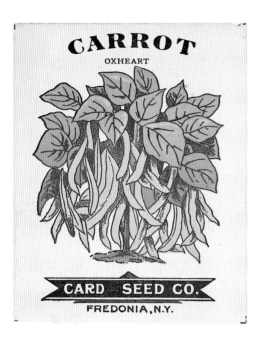

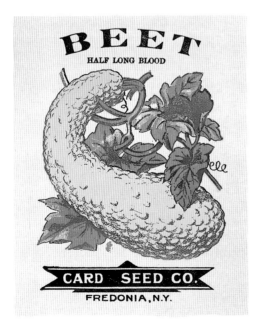

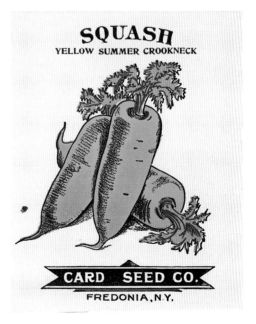

[*Seeding*] The drawings of these vegetables are so fresh it's hard to believe the seeds wouldn't still grow a plump specimen or two. With a little dexterity titles can be switched and cross-pollination can be achieved.

< 65 >

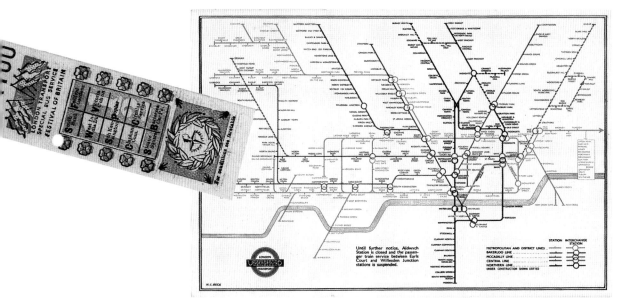

[*Travel and Tickets*] The travel industry has always put a lot of energy into advertising. Big, colorful old posters are now highly sought after and expensive, but you can still buy cheaply things like an early London Underground map or evocative old tickets to faraway places.

FACING PAGE: [*Smoking Tires*] Cigarette companies gave away a card in each packet. You could collect a whole set while you were asphyxiating yourself. This Road Safety series has a wonderful innocence about it.

< 66 >

WILLS'S
CIGARETTES

TRAFFIC SIGNALS

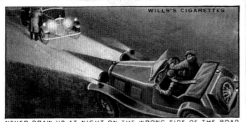

NEVER CHASE A BALL OR HOOP INTO THE ROADWAY

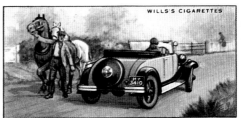

TAKE THE OFF SIDE OF THE ROAD WHEN MEETING LED HORSES

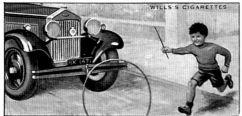

NEVER DRAW UP AT NIGHT ON THE WRONG SIDE OF THE ROAD

KEEP TO THE LEFT

OVERTAKING IN TOWNS

GETTING OUT OF TRAM LINES

[*Pre-veiling Geometry*] The simple beauty of traditional North African clothing and
the Arab fascination for geometry feel totally right together.

< 68 >

Postcards

In 1869, the Austrians issued the first postcards, and a year later the British followed suit. However, the earliest picture postcards didn't emerge till the Germans quietly started what was to become a universal trend. Without realizing it, they were setting free a torrent of images on the unsuspecting universe.

Humor, landscape, people, animals: at some point or another everything under the sun found its way onto a postcard. The cards we choose point us toward our tastes and preoccupations. I collect cards portraying North African women from the early 1900s. Why? Because I'm fascinated by their almost catlike sensuality.

Those who know the Griffin and Sabine books will realize that I not only collect postcards but also make them from scratch, like the card titled *Pre-veiling Geometry* on the facing page.

In analytical terms the postcard could almost have been designed as a model for the relationship between the conscious and the unconscious. The text deals with the day-to-day practicalities and the image represents the dreamer's world. When you look at old cards, it's curious how often the front and back express conflicting or ambiguous messages. A bold, risqué photo or illustration can be glossed over with a simple greeting: "Mildred. Sunshine wonderful. Paddling everyday. Yours, George."

In the past, postcards were often sent without any written message, just an address and a stamp. Was it that the picture was left to function as a miniature gauge of the sender's state of mind?

[*Blue Flapper*]

< 69 >

47   GRANVILLE. — *La Péche du Lançon.* —

[*Animalisms*] Collecting postcards of a particular animal, like dogs, may be popular, but personally I tend to go for the more unusual.

PREVIOUS SPREAD: [*The Seaside*] When a relatively ordinary seaside scene is enlarged, all sorts of unlikely characters come to life.

< 72 >

[*Hernia*] This guy will allmost certainly need an operation at some future date.

< 73 >

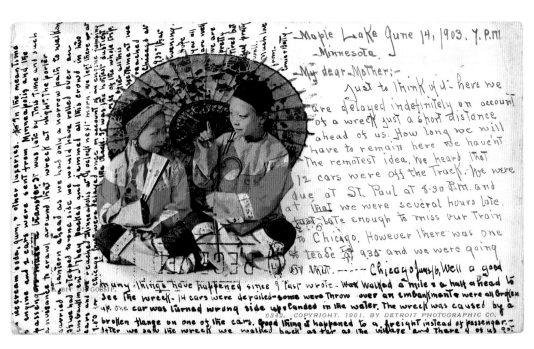

[*Back to Front*] Not everyone shies away from writing. Some folks use every available inch of space to fill in the news.

< 74 >

Boulogne-sur-Mer

Damaged by Salt Water

Type de Pêcheur.

L.L.

[*Damaged by Salt Water*] The perfect pose and a sou'wester to be proud of.

[*Blocks and Cuts*] Rubber stamps
are far from the only block
printing tools. Wood, an eraser,
and even a potato can easily be
used. This impression on hand-
made paper is taken from a
linocut.

Rubber Stamps

When I was about nine I had a John Bull printing set consisting of minute back-to-front rubber letters that had to be slotted into a wooden groove with a pair of tiny tweezers. I think I printed my name twice!

Twenty years later I received a rubber stamp of a hippo for my birthday. I refrained from uttering, "That's nice, but what the hell do I do with it?" I'd probably have thrown it in a drawer and forgotten about it if the foresighted gift-giver hadn't also included a black ink pad in the package. I stamped the hippo on a scrap of paper, then I gave it a twin, then I stamped the gas bill, then I stamped all the spare bits of paper on my table, then I stamped the back of my hand. After that I carefully put the hippo and the ink pad in a box . . . and forgot about them!

More years passed and I found them again. The ink pad had long since dried up, but I wanted to see if the hippo would work in a collage, so I bought a fresh pad and tried it out. It seemed awkward, but I could see the potential. I persisted. I tried applying it in different ways with different amounts of inking. Slowly I got the hang of how to integrate the image into the bigger picture.

My next leap came when I discovered a store that sold nothing but rubber stamps. I hate "cute," so I passed over the shelves with teddy bears and floral frippery and homed in on the odd stuff—the insects, the archaic machines, and the prewar postal cancellations of Fiji. For a while, other people's designs were ample to play with, but it was only a matter of time before I started doing my own rubber stamps. I was lucky to link up with a company that, as well as publishing my designs, is kind enough to create the one-offs I need for my books.

Of all the methods of reproduction at an artist's disposal, rubber stamps are probably the most overlooked as a serious art tool. Maybe the immediacy makes stamping seem too easy. But the truth is that a rubber stamp is like a pencil. It's not a matter of just making a mark. It's how you use it, what ground you place it on, and how you position the content in context with its surroundings.

[*Afghan Cat*]

< 77 >

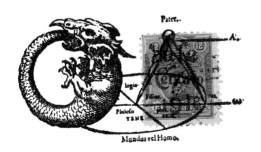

< 78 >

Registered LOST

WARNING: INADEQUATE GRAMMAR

Personal: **ABUNDANT WITH SALACIOUSNESS**

Armagedon: **last day cover**

PRECIOUS GIFT *pre-broken!*

Officially late

FRAGILE TEMPERAMENT

O.H.M.S. POSTAGE DUE

TO BE READ between THE LINES

Found curdled @ Post Office

VERY PERSONAL *resealed*

RETURNED: *inept love letter*

FACING PAGE: [*Sock-on-the-Nose*] Getting a good combination of postage stamps and rubber stamping can be hit or miss. A little to the left or right can make all the difference.

[*Wordstamps*] The post office has a tradition of stamping phrases like "returned to sender" and "damaged by crash" onto envelopes, so I decided I needed my own wordstamps.

< 79 >

[*Picturestamps*] The images I make for rubber stamps vary greatly. The quickest and often the most unusual come from joining two very different line engravings.

<small>FACING PAGE</small>: [*Philatelic Cancels*] In order to convincingly cancel an envelope, it's necessary to build a collection of rubber stamp cancellations.

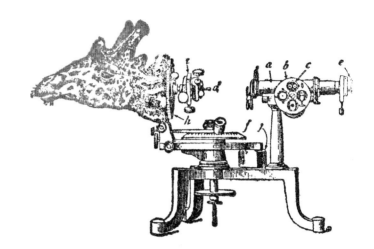

No. 83.

Fernsprechschein.

25 Pf.

für die einmalige Benutzung
des Fernsprechers.

circumscript

40 ΠΑΡ
PORTO SCRISURE
40 ΠΑΡ

30

ONE PIASTRE
POSTAGE
PAID
E·E·F 1

par Avion

ONE PENNY

4 ØRE

POSTE LOCALE
Service Mixte.
Taxe Ext.
Taxe Int. 10
TOTAL

TAHITI

ARBAH

4   3
SILVER MOON

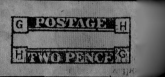

G POSTAGE H

H TWO PENCE G

AIR MAIL
SAVES
TIME AND MONEY

F.lli SANTINI

FERRARA

FABBRICA
Articoli d'illuminazione, Casalinghi e chincaglierie

MAGAZZINI
Cristallerie, Vetrerie ed accessori per illuminazione

REGISTERED

R

OFFICIEL

The E. form
from the AS. is *roun, round*, whisper:
1. A letter or character
peoples of northern Europe from

3. O
spoke
a run
hand
ber
run
run

Runes.— R
the letters carved on ston
found in Scandinavia, Scotland
Runes
ts of Europe
at similar Scandi
cryptograms c

543 - ROUEN - Cathédrale. Le pourtour du Chœur

FACING PAGE: [*Fragments*] It's well worth hanging on to ephemera scraps. You never know when they might make grounds for stamping.

[*Divergent Twins*] The colors you use and the ground you choose make a huge difference to the appearance of a rubber stamping. The two giraffes come from the same block but have a vastly different feel.

< 83 >

Photocopies

If you are nervous about working directly on a hard-found piece of ephemera, you are almost certainly going to be inhibited in your creativity. A solution to this anxiety is to photocopy the original. Black-and-white and, now, color copiers have become basic practical studio tools. You can copy a piece as many times as you wish onto thin or thick, glossy or matte paper, and then experiment with it as much as you want.

6148 SCÈNES ET TYPES – *Mauresque*. — LL.

That said, I must admit that I like to use the original artifact whenever I can. The risk of pushing too hard and losing the document or map under layers of collage gives me the same stimulative edge that I get from reading onstage.

The real fun, though, comes from copying a second image directly onto the original ephemera. That means putting the piece though the copy machine (you can run almost any paper through a copier, provided it's not going to disintegrate or jam). You may have to try a number of options in order to get the feel you are after. I tested a bunch of images over pages of antique German type before I came to the blue cow picture (page 88). Why did that one work better than other, more dynamic photos? It's not something I could have predicted—the passive pastoral scene just made its own sense.

On page 86 you'll find a photocopy (not a photograph) of an iris taped to a blueprint of a house. I pressed the flower for twenty-four hours; then, while it still had all its color, I attached it to the plan with masking tape, put it in a clear plastic sleeve, and color-copied it. It came out looking far better than I expected.

You can also copy an image onto clear film. One of the advantages of using transparent acetate is that you can lay your image over any number of backgrounds before choosing a good match. In the example on the facing page I copied one of my paintings and then looked at it transposed over a number of different carpets until I found the one that worked best.

ABOVE: [*Photo-genic*]

FACING PAGE: [*Carpet Alchemist*] Photocopy on transparency.

1½" EXPOSURE

2"x4"
STRAPPING

3"
1½"

5"

1½"
3½"
4½"

6"

8'9"4"

2" COPPER
PIPE WELDED
TO GUTTER

18½" RADIUS

" T. +G. SOFFITT FINISH

18½"

65 7
5472
9170

27"

27
54

4'6"

2'10"
4'4"   8" x 5/8" ANCHOR BOLT

2'4"4

3 2"4 FOAM PLATE
GASKET

CURVED ROOF
TT JUNCTION;
ON, FLOOR JOIST
ALL JUNCTION

2"x6" PLATE

3/4" PLYWOOD

2"x10" FLOOR PLATFORM

9'4"

8'3"4

3/4" PLYWOOD

6" x ½" ANCHOR BOLTS
STAGGERED 48" O.C.

2"x10" FLOOR
JOISTS

JOIST HANGER

FACING PAGE: [*Flat Iris*] When it comes to photocopying flowers, the trick is to press and copy them before the color drains away.

[*Scale*] The size of an image and the space it sits in should always be considered. A small image in a wide field can often create a sense of delicacy.

< 87 >

Meines Wissens sind keine vergleichenden Untersuchungen über den Fettgehalt der Gewebe der Fische gemacht, aber es will mir scheinen, daß er bei den Hochseeformen im Verhältnis zur Schwere bedeutender ist als bei den Bodenformen. Bei dem Riesenhai, den Thunfischen und ihren Verwandten ist er sehr beträchtlich, am beträchtlichsten vielleicht bei den Hornhechten, wo bisweilen die ganze Leibeshöhle neben den Eingeweiden mit Fett gefüllt ist. Die normalerweise fettreichsten Tiere und insonderheit Wirbeltiere, sind die Wale und namentlich die Bartenwale, bei denen zwar alle Organe von Fett oder Tran durchzogen sind, die inneren aber unverhältnismäßig viel weniger als die Lederhaut und das Unterhautzellgewebe. In erster Linie mag es bei diesen Tieren, denen die Behaarung bis auf ganz geringe physiologisch bedeutungslose Reschen fehlt, allerdings dem Wärmeschutz dienen, aber daneben wird es ganz gewiß in hervorragender Weise als ein Mittel, welches das spezifische Gewicht ganz bedeutend herabzusetzen imstande ist, anzusehen sein. Am wirksamsten werden da, und namentlich bei den Bartenwalen, die merkwürdigen Verhältnisse des Skelets sein, dessen Knochen, auch die langen, markröhrenlosen der Gliedmaßen, im höchsten Grade schwammig und durch und durch mit Tran durchtränkt sind. Auch die ausgestorbenen großen Reptilien (Ichthyo- und Plesiosauren), von deren Leichen vielleicht das meiste Petroleum herrührt, waren außerordentlich tranreiche, vermutlich warmblütige, pelagisch lebende Tiere; auch verschiedene, im höchsten Maße an das Leben im Meere angepaßte Vögel sind sehr reich an Fett. Die Pinguine oder Fettgänse führen ihren Namen nicht umsonst.

Eine wichtige Eigenschaft vieler Oberflächentiere des Meeres ist die Durchsichtigkeit der Gallertgewebe vieler und sehr verschiedener Formen und der Schutz, den sie dadurch haben, denn die betreffenden Tiere werden durch diese Eigenschaft tatsächlich unsichtbar, und oft verrät nur die Färbung einzelner Teile, äußerer Anhänge, der Augen u. s. w., sowie die Bewegungen ihr Vorhandensein. Man kann sich denken, daß weniges schon dem nach diesen Geschöpfen suchenden Naturforscher schwer wird, sie zu finden, ein vorüberschwimmender, räuberischer Kalmar oder Fisch, oder ein vorüberfliegender Vogel, der, sofern Hunger zur Eile anstachelt und die daher zum langen Suchen kaum Zeit haben, sie erst recht übersehen werden. Die Mehrzahl der pelagisch lebenden verschiedenen Larvenformen ist durchscheinend bis durchsichtig, am meisten wohl die durch die Wirkung von Nesselapparaten und Wehrfähigkeit nicht geschützten Rippenquallen, deren Körper trotzdem namentlich durch das prachtvolle Aufglänzen der bei jeder bewegten Ruderplättchen unter Umständen sehr bemerkbar werden, wenn auch nur bei Sonnenschein und vorübergehend. Zahlreiche pelagische Ringelwürmer, besonders aus den Familien der Alciopiden, Tomopteriden, Amphinomiden, Glyceriden, Phyllodociden u. s. w. sind durchsichtig wie Glas und verraten sich höchstens durch ihre schwarzen oder roten Augen, oder durch, nicht in jedem Ringe paarig auftretende, farbige drüsenartige Gebilde. Auch bis auf die sich deutlich markierenden Verdauungsorgane und die Augen fast völlig durchsichtige Krebse, namentlich aus der Gruppe der Garneelen, bewohnen die Oberfläche des Meeres, ebenso nicht wenige Weichtiere und sogar Kopffüßer. Die Ruder- und Kielfüßer sind bei ihrer pelagischen Lebensweise gleichfalls meist durchscheinend bis durchsichtig. Durch den Leib der 3 Zentimeter langen, schalenlosen Phyllirhoë bucephala des Mittelmeers kann man hindurchlesen.

Die an der Oberfläche der Hochsee lebenden glasigen Fische sind nur Larven und seltsamerweise gerade von auf dem Boden und zum Teil an der Küste sich aufhaltenden Formen. Leider sind diese Verhältnisse durchaus noch nicht genügend klargestellt. Man hat diese unfertigen Tiere,

[*German-Speaking Cow*] Unless an old book is of the highest quality, you are never really sure what was thrown in the original pulp. That means that any given page will respond differently. The paper in this German book is prone to magnify patches of magenta ink—one reason for choosing a magenta-free cow.

< 88 >

594 - Jeune fille juive.

[*Grid Locked*] Unlike the other images in this chapter, the young woman portrayed was fed through a computer printer. I used a page from an old stamp album and watched as the water-based ink fixed on the white surface but was rejected by the blue, oil-based grid lines.

[*Parchment*] A drawing executed
on parchment paper can be
gentle on the eyes. This drawing of a plane and butterfly
uses a combination of colored
pencil and graphite.

Drawings

Anyone who has tried to assemble a piece of furniture from an instruction sheet composed by a dyslexic, Scandinavian sadist knows what panic is. I've noticed that as soon as the word drawing gets mentioned, many people take on a similar look of petrified hopelessness. Unlike the example of the unjoinable joinery, drawing has become such a daunting challenge for obvious reasons. Quite simply, the art of seeing is seldom taught in schools. Drawing has pretty much been deemed a redundant activity unless a person is "artistic" and headed for art college.

I cannot overcome anyone's fear of drawing. A fear that was probably fixed in the first instant by a combination of exercises in telegraph-pole perspective and enforced periods of sitting in front of a bowl of fruit waiting for it to transmogrify itself onto paper. Instead, I'm going to try to stimulate those who want to play a little.

If you want to draw something that you have a good reference for, don't be shy about using a light table or even a windowpane. To add extra interest to a drawing, place a piece of ephemera directly over your reference picture, put light behind it, and trace the image onto the ephemera's surface. Don't get hung up on always having to draw from scratch. Certainly it's a skill I encourage in the long term, but at the start, functionality is the key. Even Canaletto used a camera obscura to project the canals of Venice directly onto his studio desktop.

There are so many different ways to draw. Some require a facility for rendering, but others almost work better without it. The petroglyph drawings on page 95 are done with a tiny dipping pen dragged shakily over a rough, uncontrollable surface, whereas the charcoal face on newspaper (page 94) was more like a therapeutic outburst.

[*Pointillizing a Mummified Cat*]

< 91 >

< 92 >

FACING PAGE: [*Parrot on the Fly*] To make a drawing look old, coat the paper with strong tea. If you wanted to speed up the aging process, subject the paper alternately to cold and dark, and then heat and light. But the simplest way to make a drawing appear old is to do it on an old book flyleaf.

[*Fancy Dress*] In the introduction I described this Italian invoice as a concept. Does its reality (albeit an invention) enlighten or confuse historical reliability?

< 93 >

[*Graphic Journalism*] Drawing with charcoal and compressed charcoal directly onto yellowed newspaper can give an image an extra dimension of texture and implied context.

FACING PAGE: [*Petroglyphs*] Not all drawing needs be done dry with pencil or charcoal. For example, a black ink brush drawing can be effective when laid over colored tissue saturated in matte medium.

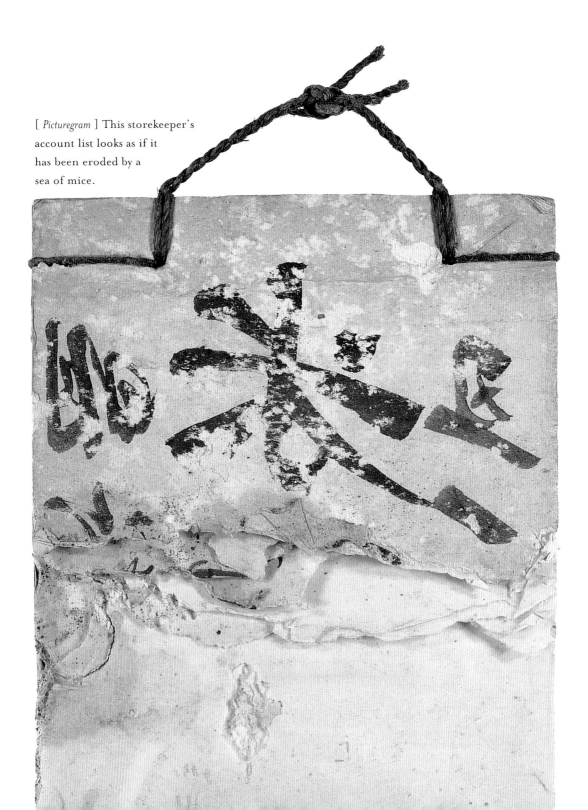

[*Picturegram*] This storekeeper's account list looks as if it has been eroded by a sea of mice.

Handwriting and Type

At one time, handwriting was commonplace and the literate were adept at reading it. Eyes were attuned to comprehend individualistic styles and letter formations; the handwritten word was a reflection of an individual's personality. You could establish whether your correspondent was tight and careful or open and gregarious by the letters shaped by his or her pen.

Now, for reasons of expedience, we teach a uniformly constructed alphabet and non-self-expressive handwriting.

When the mechanical writing revolution came first with the typewriter and then the computer, fewer and fewer people felt a need to handwrite. And those who did were faced with readers who had little patience and expected instant legibility. It is hardly surprising then that today we look with abstract awe at what seems to be the swirling complexities of an everyday hand from one hundred fifty years ago. It could be said that calligraphy keeps the practice of handwriting alive, but it seems to me that calligraphy is a more conscious act—a precise and formal kind of script that is usually perceived as a decorative craft. As much as I admire calligraphy, I'd rather see natural handwriting that takes pleasure in its eccentricity and informal beauty.

Typography has been around for more than half a millennium. From wooden block to metal press to Lettraset and golf-ball typewriters, the march of the preformed alphabet has been inexorable. In its own way, type is extremely pleasing to the eye. There are more typefaces than visible stars in the night sky, and they offer the artist a vast array of shapes and forms to tinker with. For me the most fascinating aspect of type apart from the pure letter shaping is the relationship of one letter to another. Whether floating around on a page or lined up for legibility, every letter in every alphabet has a relative, comfortable distance from the previous one. A *t* next to an *o* requires a different spacing than a *t* next to a *w*. There is no formula that can be applied to all letters and all faces.

РЕПИША

МАЛАЯ

КИНЕМАТОГРАФИИ

ПРЕДСТАВИТЕЛИ СОВРЕМЕННЫХ ГРУППИРОВОК

ВЫСТУПЯТ:

Are our souls stranded, unable to express themselves in a suitable language? We don't dream in words: our imaginations are picture-based. Images are multi-faceted, & often combined with others of them like, offer multiple possibilities that become so dense they are only negotiable by means of intuition. They are nonquantifiable, therefore they appear to be unreliable. That's why our overt commitment to linear logic moves us away from an understanding of images. We word which we can define. But we are text, we settled. adults never properly heard this

is hardly surprising, as we have become separated from the pictures that are the wellsprings of our being. It would seem that few people today feel truly comfortable with images — our dream

[*The Illustrated Letter*] If you choose to illustrate a letter, you can work around the image . . . or go through it.

FACING PAGE: [*Russian Fish*] When rough-cut text is blown up many times its original size, the edges will take on a pleasing asymmetry.

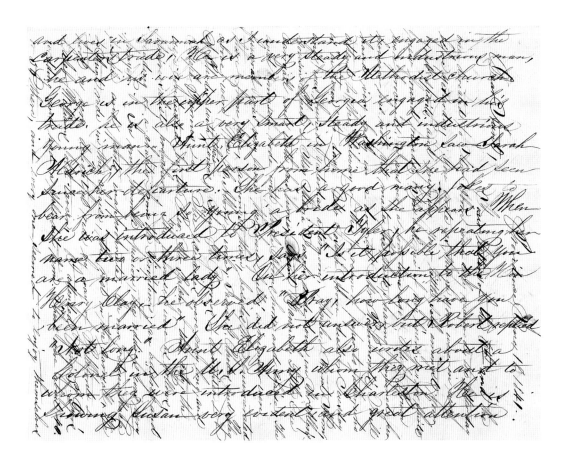

[*Two-Way Handwriting*] It's surprising how legible script traveling both ways at once can actually be.

FACING PAGE: [*Words and Numbers*] I'd never used gold leaf till I attempted this typographical experiment. The ground is made of odd scraps of typographic ephemera, followed by acrylic stain, then the gold, and finally a transparent overlay of a Spanish map and an inverted 2.

< 100 >

[*Gumshoe*] An enlarged playing
card of a trilby-touting sleuth
from an unknown game
(1940s).

< 102 >

Games

I guess all those hours as a kid playing with jigsaws, dominoes, playing cards, and chessmen are what has led me to include a chapter on games. I even used to invent games: making the rules, cutting out bits of cards, designing the money.

Old games cover an amazingly wide spectrum from the cheaply printed ones on low-grade cardboard to the ornate, delicate, and highly expensive. Some come in boxes with single elements missing and some turn up as single, isolated pieces devoid of packaging and rules. I love these markers whose surfaces have been oiled and rounded by touch. They emanate a foot soldier's sense of purpose.

I hunt for games all over, yet I've bought most of the best ones at garage sales. While they can be purchased from antique stores and off the Web, I find it much more satisfying to stumble onto an early bingo game or a pack of Old Maid amongst someone's cracked teacups and armless Barbies. Once you start rooting around, you'll find all kinds of interesting game material in unexpected corners. In a fishing tackle box at a yard sale, I came across three wooden Scrabble letters and the metal top hat from an old Monopoly set—I'm still trying to work out the angler's intent! If I can infuse that kind of curiosity of connection into my artwork, I'll be perfectly happy.

[Down-at-Heel Old Rook Box]

[*Bingo*] Putting together the box cover and the inwards of this old bingo game, I imagined someone was staring at it and being reminded of a wet afternoon from their childhood when they sat on a living room floor waiting for their number to come up.

FACING PAGE: [*Spread Hand*] The broken deck of cards I bought in Camden Passage, London. The stretched green baize came from a cloth shop on Pender Street, Vancouver.

< 104 >

[*Blackpool Tower*] I bought this jigsaw on eBay knowing there was a piece missing. I put it together, took out a few more bits, and then inserted a playing card of a giant stuffed gorilla from the 1933 Chicago World's Fair.

PREVIOUS SPREAD, LEFT:
[*Die Cast*] I'd been picking up the old dice for a while before I realized I had a collection. This handful of dice was thrown across a painting of the pyramids seen from on high.

PREVIOUS SPREAD, RIGHT:
[*Code*] Even though the placement of these old Chinese dominoes was random, it seems like there must be a mathematical cipher running through the order of spots.

[*Alger 19*] Invoiced postcard.

Collage

I have left collage until last because it is the sum of all the previous chapters. Every technique and every combination of ideas can be incorporated within collage, and only paint need be added to visually hold the parts together.

The method and practice of collage tend to encourage swiftness, but the speed with which layers can be built can also serve as a trapdoor to a chaotic mess. As fast as you can create a vital collage, it can also collapse under you. One minute everything is looking good, the next the various elements have lost their sense of relationship and become a muddle, like too many colors mixed together into a grungy brown.

I prefer to use fragments rather than whole pieces of found material, which means my pictures tend to be small. Large collages may be quick eye-catchers, but they are often easily glanced over. When a picture has to be approached and observed closely, the viewer is pulled into a world that demands committed inspection.

These smaller collages tend to need more nurturing, and when I finish the preliminary stages of assemblage I go back into the picture with a small brush and carefully rework and retouch any harsh or uncomfortable edges. This merging stops the eye from jarring and allows the viewer to see the work as a continuous piece rather than a series of partially related sections.

Anyone can slap a collage onto paper—only time and practice will allow you the skills and understanding to elevate your expression into one of dialogue and harmony. Developing a technical knowledge can help, but technique alone won't make a worthy collage. Keep in mind the content, but don't be too literal. And always allow yourself the freedom to experiment without losing sight of the need to compose.

[*Fish and Cherub Collage*]

[*The Drummer*] An oil painting of a young woman's face I did in the 1970s. Looking at it again recently, I felt as if it had come from the period around the First World War, so I attached the wooden soldier to help fix the collage in time.

FACING PAGE: [*Garden of the Fallen Angels*] I was drawn by the *Shadowland* cover, and it reminded me of the remains of the bird that one of my daughters found.

< 112 >

< 113 >

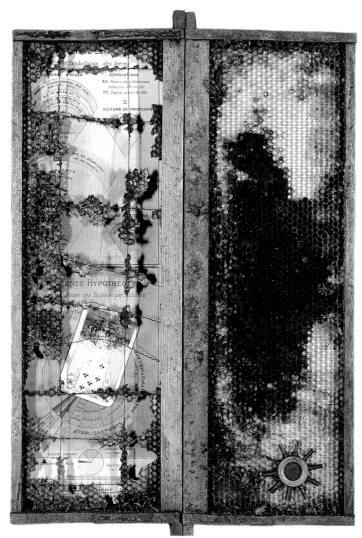

LEFT: [*Double Honeycomb*] Once in a while (not nearly often enough), a work will emerge out of nowhere. I found the honeycomb frames at a garage sale, joined them together, and added two painted book pages, a playing card, and a watchmaker's sprocket. It all came together in a matter of minutes.

FACING PAGE: [*The Kingdom*] This collage is a "show-off" piece. Explaining how I put it together would take years. Applying the paint and found material cannot be done to formula—you have to employ your eye, your heart, your gut, and your slow-learned craft. Materials used here include printed scraps (fifty plus), acrylic paint, watercolor, ink, gold powder, colored pencil, glue, matte medium, and tissue paper.

< 115 >

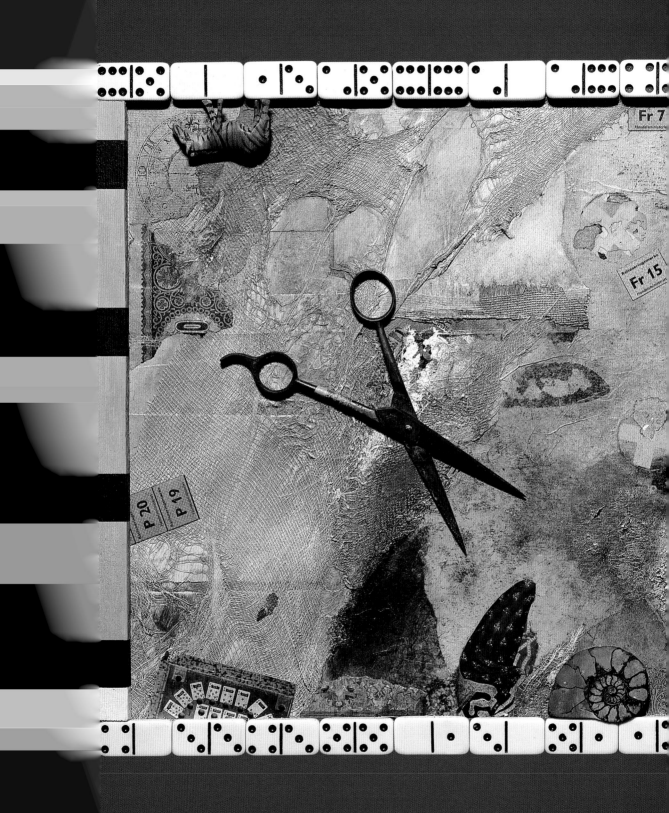

[*Zebra Trail*] Unlike *Double Honeycomb*, this collage had to be fought for every inch of the way. It took weeks of sheer slog to find the right style and tone. Locating the scissors alone took days and days of searching in junk and antique stores.

Player's Cigarettes

Modern Game,
Black-breasted
Reds

разрядъ

ГОСУДАРС

ВНУТРЕННІЙ 4½% ВЫИГ

и на основаніи постановленія Време